MEET CRYSTAL

A self-proclaimed "digital missionary" Crystal has always dreamed of her perfect career, climbing the corporate ladder, and achieving success. And she did – and then God began redefining hustle, taking Crystal on a journey from striving to serving. From corporate America to non-profits and freelance work, Crystal understands the tempting pull of striving but has learned to lean into the blessing of focusing her hustle toward serving God's kingdom.

A self-employed mama to a 6-year-old (and married to her high school sweetheart), Crystal is passionate about cultivating a community where faith and friendship come together. Author of "Creative Basics: 30 Days to Awesome Social Media Art," creator of the popular "Clarity Coaching" Course, editor of "Craving Connection" and host of the annual Write 31 Days challenge, Crystal writes regularly at crystalstine.me or on Instagram @crystalstine.

CONTENTS

About this study

It is my prayer that this study would serve as a tool to encourage you to work hard without shame and rest well without guilt as we follow God's example of hustle. I call it "holy hustle" – the kind of work that honors others, helps us become good stewards of our gifts, and builds God's Kingdom instead of our own.

How to use this study

Each week you'll find a section of Scripture to focus on, a brief devotional, and 5 days of personal study questions and activities designed to help you dig deeper into God's Word (instead of focusing on my words). Write in this book, fold over pages, doodle in the margins, highlight it – whatever you need to do! You'll want to make sure you have a Bible nearby (a study Bible will be super handy), your favorite pen, and – if you'd like – a few friends who want to go on this *Holy Hustle* adventure too.

What is Holy Hustle?

A few years ago I was sitting in church, listening to our pastor talk about the story of Ruth. As we read along in our Bibles (or, on our Bible apps), I skipped ahead. You see, I thought I knew this story already.

"She came and has been on her feet since early morning, except that she rested a little in the shelter."
Ruth 2:7, CSB

But I had no idea what God was about to do with it. Sometimes it's hard to read familiar passages of the Bible and stay focused.

We think we know what's going to happen next, and we assume that anything we've learned in the past is all that there is to learn.

But God's Word is living and powerful, which means that the same Bible stories can take us to new places in our faith, depending on our age, season of life, or even the circumstances of our day.

As I skipped ahead in Ruth's story – during a season where work, loss, striving, and balance were at the forefront of my mind – I found myself learning something new.

Ruth hustled.

As she went to the fields to work, she worked hard. She was recognized and set apart because of her hard work. She worked until the job was done, rested, and then continued to glean in those fields for weeks. Ruth's motivation was to honor God by supporting her family. God's plan was to include her in the family line of Jesus.

It made me wonder what else God had to say about work and rest, and started me on an unexpected adventure as I discovered what "holy hustle" might look like in our lives.

Day 1
Read Genesis 1 – 2:3

Week 1

Work hard, rest well.

Although the inspiration for *Holy Hustle* came from the book of Ruth, we're going to start our journey together at the very beginning – learning how God models work and rest for us in Genesis. We need to take some time to make sure we understand what God has to say about this topic before we start talking about what it looks like in our lives. We'll also spend a little time this week considering what "hustle" means and assessing where we currently fall on the striving/serving – laziness/rest scale. Knowing what God says and understanding where we need His help will prepare us to be open to the work He wants to do in our lives.

> *"God saw all that he had made, and it was very good indeed."*
> *Genesis 1:31*

Who wrote the book of Genesis?

What are the themes of Genesis?

When was it written?

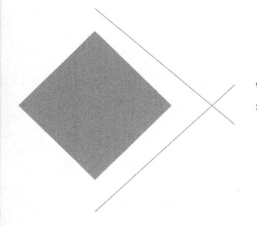

What do you hope to learn from our study of Genesis this week?

Day 2

Read Genesis 1 – 2:3 again (if you'd like, choose a different translation to see if it helps you focus if this is a familiar passage).

1.   What do you initially take away from your reading today?

2.   What does this section of Scripture teach us about God?

Day 2

3. How does this Scripture come alive in a new way as you read it through a "holy hustle" lens?

Good and Holy
Genesis 1 – 2:3

As we read through this short section of Genesis, ask God to show you the ways He wants you to learn work and rest from His model. In six days God worked hard (one could say He hustled) until the job was complete – a job that took an incredible, never before seen amount of creativity. When He was done, He called it good.

And then, when everything was finished according to His plan, He rested – and called it holy.

When we work hard, putting our plans, agendas, and tasks in God's hands and trust Him with the details, we can work hard until the job is done, and then rest well, knowing we have honored Him with our efforts.

Day 3

Read John 1:1-5

1. How does this Scripture connect with what we read yesterday in Genesis?

2. We already looked at when Genesis was written. When was John written? How many years have passed since each of these books of the Bible were written?

Day 3

3. How would you paraphrase (rewrite in your own words) today's Scripture?

John 1:1-5
The Message

The Word was first, the Word present to God, God present to the Word. The Word was God, in readiness for God from day one. Everything was created through him;
 nothing—not one thing!—
 came into being without him.
What came into existence was Life, and the Life was Light to live by. The Life-Light blazed out of the darkness; the darkness couldn't put it out.

Read Genesis 1 – 2:3

1. Take a moment to list everything God DID in these verses.

2. If we had a scale in front of us that had "holy hustle" in the center, "striving" to the left, and "laziness" to the right, where are you in this current season?

Day 4

3. If, like most of us, you aren't quite in that sweet spot of working hard AND resting well, what tends to push you along that scale? Emotions, circumstances, expectations, or fear are just a few examples.

"Tucked into holy hustle is freedom that takes away the guilt of work and the shame of rest."

- Holy Hustle, chapter 1 -

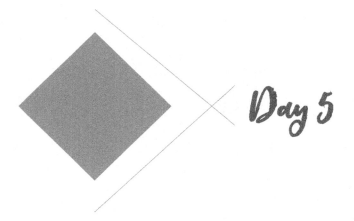

Day 5

Read Genesis 1 – 2:3

1. Write down your definition of the word "hustle." Now, look up "hustle" in the dictionary. How has your personal definition been impacted by society or culture?

2. Based purely on the dictionary definition of hustle, how do God's actions in Genesis 1-2:3 model "hustle"?

Day 5

3. What, in your mind, would transform your typical, every day, striving version of "hustle" into something holy? How is God asking you to change how you work, or rest, as a result?

"At the end of the day, *hustle* is simply a word that exemplifies hard work and effort, but I bet many of us would define it differently. Does "ceaselessly striving" sound familiar? "

Holy Hustle, chapter 1

When I was growing up, I had big dreams of becoming a magazine editor in New York City. I was never the kind of girl who planned out her wedding, or had dreams about her future family, but I did have dreams and plans for my career. As I've considered what, in the past, has sent me spiraling toward striving or leaning into laziness, one of the biggest triggers occurs when my dreams feel derailed. When I was fired from the job I thought I would have forever, I went into survival (and striving) mode. When the rejections piled up, I escaped into the laziness that is binge watching too many shows. This week we'll look at what God can do with a detour – and maybe change how we feel about failure along the way.

> "God sent me ahead of you to establish you
> as a remnant within the land and to keep
> you alive by a great deliverance."
> *Genesis 45:7*

Summarize the story of Joseph in your own words.

How much of this story were you familiar with before reading today?

How does this section of Genesis connect with last week's reading?

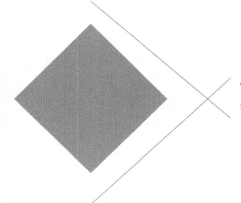

**What do you hope to learn from our
study of Joseph's story this week?**

Day 2

Read Genesis 37 and 39 - 45 again (if you'd like, choose a different translation to see if it helps you focus if this is a familiar passage).

1. What do you initially take away from your reading today?

2. What does this section of Scripture teach us about God?

Day 2

3. How does this Scripture come alive in a new way as you read it through a "holy hustle" lens?

The Lord's Favor

Don't be discouraged by the length of this week's reading. Joseph's story is an encouraging example of how God's plans are better than our own — even when we don't understand what is going on.

Joseph had dreams — literally — about what God had promised to do in his life, but I doubt the path to get there looked anything like he'd hoped. And yet, because of Joseph's love for God, he served and worked humbly, honoring God with his actions. And, in the end, Joseph saw how God kept His promises.

Along the way, Joseph connected with people, used his talents, and grew into the man God knew he would become. When we rush to make our plans and dreams happen in our own time, we often miss the opportunities God gives us to learn, grow, and connect.

Day 3

Read 2 Corinthians 3:5

1. How does this Scripture connect with what we read yesterday in Genesis?

2. What dreams are on your heart right now? How does this verse help you stay within that sweet spot of "holy hustle" as you work toward them?

Day 3

3. How would you paraphrase (rewrite in your own words) today's Scripture?

2 Corinthians 3:5
The Voice

"Don't be mistaken; in and of ourselves we know we have little to offer, but any competence *or value* we have comes from God."

Read Genesis 37 and 39-45

1. Take a moment and list where Joseph started, where he ended, and any perceived "failures" that happened in his story.

2. How would you define "failure"? Have you ever experienced a time when God used a failure in your life to move you to the next step on His path for your life?

Day 4

3. Think about a time when you gave up on chasing your God-given dreams because of failure. If you had viewed those setbacks as stepping stones instead of stumbling blocks, how differently would you have responded?

"We're meant to make God famous."

— Holy Hustle, chapter 1 —

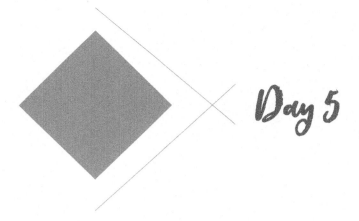

Day 5

Read Genesis 39:1-6

1. Read today's section of Joseph's story and list the blessings that occurred because "the Lord was with Joseph."

2. Instead of giving up when his dreams took a detour, Joseph continued to faithfully serve God. How did this decision bless the people in Joseph's life?

Day 5

3. List anything from this week's readings that have helped change your definition of failure. When your dreams take a detour, how will this help you remain faithful to the work God has called you to do?

"Holy hustle means standing firm and taking up the space God has called you to, choosing a life of faith, even if it never brings fame."

Holy Hustle, chapter 3

The Bible is full of wonderful examples of faithful men and women who remained obedient to God in good and bad times. This week, however, we're going to take a look at what happens when our daily obedience – those simple moments of "yes, Lord" – result in surprise blessings. Jobs that we never thought we wanted suddenly become the work we knew we were created to do. Children we never dreamed of having suddenly become an answer to a prayer we didn't know we needed. Opportunities that fall through suddenly create space for a joy-filled moment we might have otherwise missed. And who better to study this week than Mary?

Who wrote the book of Luke?

When was it written?

What are the themes of Luke?

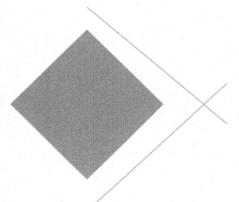

What do you hope to learn from our study of Mary this week?

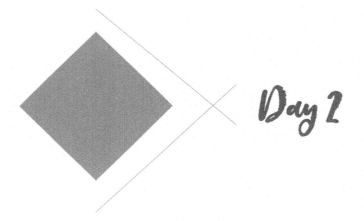

Day 2

Read Luke 1:26-55 again (if you'd like, choose a different translation to see if it helps you focus if this is a familiar passage).

1.   What do you initially take away from your reading today?

2.   What does this section of Scripture teach us about God?

Day 2

3. How does this Scripture come alive in a new way as you read it through a "holy hustle" lens?

Inviting God to Surprise Us
Luke 1:26-55

I don't know about you, but I'm not usually a fan of surprises. I like to know what's going to happen, when it's going to happen, and how I'm supposed to dress for the occasion. I nearly ruined my husband's proposal because I was so caught off guard, and I never know where to look or what to do when a group yells "surprise!" as I walk into a room.

It's pretty likely that I wouldn't have responded to Gabriel's news the same way Mary did. But Mary's faithfulness and her habit of daily obedience to God gave her the courage to say, "May it be done." And so, she invited God to surprise her with an unexpected blessing that would change the world.

Day 3

Read Matthew 1:18-25

1. How does this Scripture compare with what we read
    yesterday in Luke? List the similarities and differences.

2. Take some time to answer the same questions about
    Matthew that we answered about Luke. Who wrote it?
    When was it written? What are the themes?

Day 3

3. How would you paraphrase (rewrite in your own words) today's Scripture?

Mathew 1:24
CSB

"When Joseph woke up, he did as the Lord's angel had commanded him."

Read Luke 1:26-55

1. Take a moment and write down how you would have reacted if you had been in Mary's position.

2. Think about your reaction to surprises in your life. Do you make room for the unexpected in your work and rest, or do you try to fill every moment with plans and purpose?

Day 4

3. How would your approach to your work or rest (your "holy hustle") be different if you took some time each morning to invite God to surprise and delight you through your daily obedience?

"Holy hustle means a small obedience with our gifts and a willingness to work with others can make a significant impact in God's kingdom."

— Holy Hustle, chapter 3 —

Day 5

Read Luke 1:26-55

1. Read today's section of Mary's story and list the surprises that occurred because she said "yes" to God's plan for her life.

2. In verses 46-55, Mary worships God with a song, thanking Him for inviting her to be a part of the story He was writing for humanity. Rewrite Mary's song into your own words, with your own story.

Day 5

3. List anything from this week's readings that have helped change how you view surprises. When the unexpected happens, how will you respond differently next time?

"Holy hustle means understanding the part of the work we're responsible for and stepping out of the way to let God do His part."

Holy Hustle, chapter 4

I've been known to be a bit of a perfectionist, and making mistakes has never been easy for me. Small mistakes – like sending an email with the wrong date in it, or forgetting to send my daughter's library book back to school – are embarrassing. Big mistakes – the kind that have had people unfriend me, ask me to resign, or consider me unworthy for an opportunity – are devastating. The pain associated with big mistakes makes me even more afraid to make small errors. But, as we'll learn this week from Paul, God has a plan for us, and work for us to do, even when we do make mistakes – as long as we learn to move through them.

Who wrote the book of Acts?

When was it written?

What are the themes of Acts?

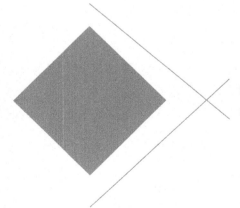

What do you hope to learn from our
study of Paul this week?

Day 2

Read Acts 9:1-30 again (if you'd like, choose a different translation to see if it helps you focus if this is a familiar passage).

1.   What do you initially take away from your reading today?

2.   What does this section of Scripture teach us about God?

Day 2

3. How does this Scripture come alive in a new way as you read it through a "holy hustle" lens?

Moving Through Our Mistakes
Acts 9:1-30

Have you ever been so afraid to make a mistake that you were frozen in place? Maybe your work required learning a new skill and you didn't want to let anyone down. Or you were asked to do something or serve in some way that you just KNEW you wouldn't be able to do.

Or maybe you've struggled to overcome people's perceptions and judgements of you long after you've allowed God to change your heart. They still see you in the old way, remembering your past, your failures, your mistakes – while you are ready and willing to honor God with your work. If only they would include you.

We all make mistakes, mess up, and make the wrong choices – but God still has work for us to do! When we stop putting our pride ahead of our love for Jesus, we can do incredible things for God's Kingdom.

Look at the author of Romans, 1 & 2 Corinthians, Galatians, Ephesians, Philippians, Colossians, 1 & 2 Thessalonians, 1 & 2 Timothy, Titus, and Philemon.

1. Who is the author attributed to these 13 books of the Bible?

2. How does this knowledge, along with what we learned about Saul yesterday, affect how you think God feels about wrong choices?

Day 3

3. Finish this sentence: "If God can do all that through Paul, after what he'd done, then surely He can _____ _____ in my life!

Titus 3:5
CSB

"He saved us – not by works of righteousness that we had done, but according to his mercy – through the washing of regeneration and renewal by the Holy Spirit."

Read Acts 9:1-30

1. Take a moment and write down any mistakes you've been
    dwelling on (specifically related to your work or rest).

2. Consider Paul's incredible story. What would have been
    different if he had doubted the work God had given him to
    do?

Day 4

3. How would your work-hard, rest-well life be different if you decided to learn from – instead of dwell on – your mistakes, trusting that God has put you in this place for a specific reason?

"I'd spent so much time trying not to get hit by closing doors that I lost the ability to see the open doors God was putting in my path."

– Holy Hustle, chapter 6 –

Day 5

Read Acts 9:1-30

1. Read today's section of Paul's story and list the ways his new life exemplifies "holy hustle."

2. Write about a time when you've had trouble believing someone had truly changed – or when others have doubted the transformation in your life.

Day 5

3. List anything from this week's readings that have helped change how you view God's ability to use you – despite your mistakes. When you make wrong choices in the future, how will you respond differently?

"Holy hustle is about changing our thinking from "What's in it for me?" to "How can I serve?"

Holy Hustle, chapter 6

Do you remember the exercise we did back on Week 1, Day 4 where we identified where we were on the "holy hustle" scale? Let's quickly do that again. Are you in the same place, or have you moved? There are any number of reasons that we might find ourselves sliding on that scale (even on a daily basis!), but identifying those triggers will help us know when to adjust our work and our rest. Sometimes we'll find ourselves striving because of outward pressures, or internal expectations. Maybe a circumstance with a friend makes us avoid our responsibilities, or doubt that we can make a difference. If we can identify what sends us sliding, maybe we can stop giving it such control over our lives.

> *"My heart rejoices in the Lord."*
> *1 Samuel 2:1*

Who wrote the book of 1 Samuel?

When was it written?

What are the themes of 1 Samuel?

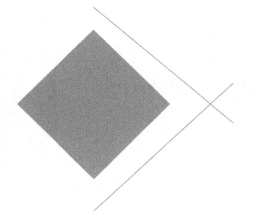

What do you hope to learn from our study this week?

Day 2

Read 1 Samuel 1 – 2:10 again (if you'd like, choose a different translation to see if it helps you focus if this is a familiar passage).

1.   What do you initially take away from your reading today?

2.   What does this section of Scripture teach us about God?

Day 2

3. How does this Scripture come alive in a new way as you read it through a "holy hustle" lens?

Identifying Our Triggers
1 Samuel 1 – 2:10

Can I tell you one very real, very honest trigger that sends me flying out of "holy hustle" and into striving or laziness?

Comparison.

When I look around at what she's doing, what they have, or what she has been invited to do, I typically do one of two things. I either scramble, or I hide. I decide to stop waiting on God and start working to build up my own kingdom, or I throw in the towel and figure "why bother?"

As we read another story like Hannah's this week, my prayer is that our eyes would not only be opened to the stumbling block we need to watch for, but that our feet would find themselves firmly planted right where God has us — following His model of work and rest.

Read Genesis 30:1-24

1. How does this Scripture connect with what we read
    yesterday in 1 Samuel?

2. What role do comparison and envy play in these stories?
    What role have they played in your own holy hustle
    journey?

Day 3

3. Take some time today to pray and ask God to show you what triggers in your life send you reeling away from His plan for your life.

1 Samuel 1:15
CSB

"I've been pouring out my heart before the Lord."

Read 1 Samuel 1 – 2:10

1.   We've addressed comparison as a trigger that might send
     some of us out of the sweet spot of holy hustle, but what
     are some others? Consider external sources (world events,
     natural disasters, finances, etc) and internal (stress, family
     holidays, anxiety, etc.).

2.   What does our reaction to these triggers tell us about how
     much we trust (or doubt) the work God has given us to do?

Day 4

3. How would your work-hard, rest-well life be different if you were able to identify your triggers, see them coming, and respond differently? How would your ability to serve God and His people change?

"In holy hustle, putting others first isn't a problem; it's the whole point."

— Holy Hustle, chapter 7 —

Day 5

Read 1 Samuel 1 – 2:10

1. Read Hannah's story again today and list the ways she worked hard AND rested well (or waited on God).

2. Take a few moments to list different types of work you do, and then see if you can identify any triggers that are specific to that work. Ask God to help you stand firm when facing those challenges.

Day 5

3. List anything from this week's readings that have helped provide clarity about why you might find yourself striving or feeling lazy, and how this knowledge will help you respond differently in the future.

"Although we might be the last ones to cross the finish line, our hustle is no less holy than the one who crossed first."

— *Holy Hustle, chapter 8* -

When I first started to think about this message of *Holy Hustle*, I tried to identify why I was struggling to reconcile work and rest. I love working and using my gifts, but I felt ashamed to admit it in faith-based circles. And rest? It doesn't look like quiet rooms and candles and soft music for me, and I felt guilty when I tried to make it look that way and – inevitably – failed. I also knew that the hustle message I was reading from our culture – the climb over everyone, be the best, never stop version – wasn't right either. Ultimately, holy hustle brought the two together for me, not only with God's model in Genesis but with the reminders throughout Scripture that we are called to a life of faith in ACTION.

Who wrote the book of Matthew?

When was it written?

What are the themes of Matthew?

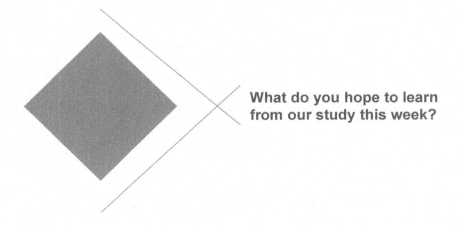

**What do you hope to learn
from our study this week?**

Read Matthew 28:16-20 again (if you'd like, choose a different translation to see if it helps you focus if this is a familiar passage).

1.   What do you initially take away from your reading today?

2.   What does this section of Scripture teach us about God?

Day 2

3. How does this Scripture come alive in a new way as you read it through a "holy hustle" lens?

Faith in Action
Matthew 28:16-20

This very last section of the book of Matthew is called "The Great Commission." After spending years traveling with Jesus, the disciples had recently witnessed His crucifixion – and now, resurrection. In Matthew 28:10 Jesus instructs the disciples to head to a mountain in Galilee, where He met with them.

After years serving, healing, ministering, and living alongside Jesus, I imagine they might have been wondering….."Now what?" And so, Jesus assures them of His authority and instructs them to go and make disciples of nations (v19).

Go. Make. This is faith in action, working together to grow God's Kingdom (for His glory, not our own).

Day 3

Read James 2:14-26

1. How does this Scripture connect with what we read yesterday in Matthew?

2. How do faith and action (in this case "works") go together? If this passage of Scripture feels confusing, try reading it in The Message.

Day 3

3. What ways have you experienced work without faith, or faith without work? How is your experience different when they're combined?

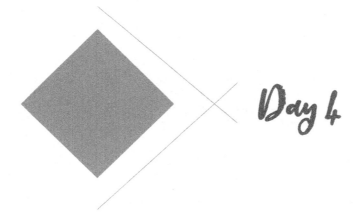

Read Matthew 28:16-20

1. How does this reading of The Great Commission change how you view holy hustle?

2. When we consider the ways in which work and faith are connected, how do you feel? Are you relieved that you can work without shame as you honor God with your gifts, or do you feel overwhelmed - like you've just added more to your to-do list?

Day 4

3. How would your work-hard, rest-well life be different if you were able to approach holy hustle as "faith in action"?

"God will use every piece of our story to illuminate His glory."

– Holy Hustle, chapter 9 –

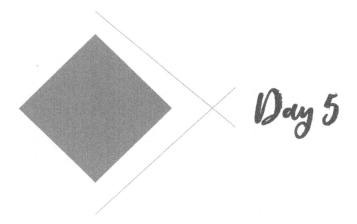

Read Matthew 28:16-20

1. Read The Great Commission again today and list the action words in this passage of Scripture.

2. Make a list of the people you interact with every day, week, and month. What are some practical ways that you can serve them, combining faith and work to honor The Great Commission?

Day 5

3. List anything from this week's readings that have helped you reconcile work, rest, and faith in your own heart.

"Become captivated by God's purpose in your life and lean into the work hard, rest well, and live the life of holy hustle God has called you to, right where you are."

—Holy Hustle, chapter 8 -

Day 1
Read Hebrews 11

Week 7

Recognition.

In my former career as an Assistant Vice President in Marketing, our team sat down and took some complicated personality surveys to find out what motivated us. Was it money? Rewards? Status?

For me, it was recognition. Public recognition, to be precise. I wanted all the credit that was due me, and I wanted everyone to know how awesome I was. Is it any surprise God wanted to remove that job, and those idols, from my life? This week we're going to explore the kind of recognition that SHOULD motivate us – the kind that comes from God, for a job well done for His Kingdom.

> *"Now faith is the reality of what is hoped for, the proof of what is not seen."*
> *Hebrews 11:1*

Who wrote the book of Hebrews?

When was it written?

What are the themes of Hebrews?

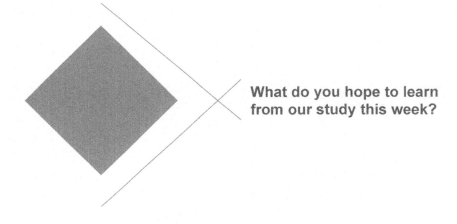

What do you hope to learn
from our study this week?

Day 2

Read Hebrews 11 again (if you'd like, choose a different translation to see if it helps you focus if this is a familiar passage).

1.   What do you initially take away from your reading today?

2.   What does this section of Scripture teach us about God?

Day 2

3. How does this Scripture come alive in a new way as you read it through a "holy hustle" lens?

Heavenly Recognition vs. Human Praise
Hebrews 11

As we read through the list of men and women in what is commonly referred to as the "Hall of Faith," we can forget that most of them never received the kind of recognition on earth that we might expect.

We would expect someone on this list today to have hundreds of thousands of social media followers, a book deal, television appearances, and probably an apparel line in Target.

But these men and women are honored for their faith. Their every day, ordinary obedience to God is what set them apart. They made mistakes, their stories weren't perfectly curated to hide their errors, and yet they were chosen by God and honored Him with their lives — even when it meant, for most of them, never seeing the results of that obedience while they were alive.

Day 3

Read Mark 8:36-37

1. How does this Scripture connect with what we read yesterday in Hebrews?

2. What connection have you seen in your own life between a need for public recognition and pride?

Day 3

3. Take some time to pray, asking God to reveal your motivation behind your work. Is it to honor and glorify God, or is it for public recognition and accolades? Write today's passage down, keeping it near your work space as a reminder as we go forward.

Mark 8:36
The Message

"You're not in the driver's seat; *I* am. Don't run from suffering; embrace it. Follow me and I'll show you how. Self-help is no help at all. "

Day 4

Read Hebrews 11

1. Read through the list of actions associated with the men and women in Hebrews 11 and write down the ones that stand out to you.

2. Imagine that your name has been added to the Hall of Faith. How would you write your own "By faith" sentence?

Day 4

3. How would your work-hard, rest-well life be different if you were able to stop relying on likes, follows, and public recognition and instead find peace knowing that God is aware of all that we do?

"Holy hustle means using your light to brighten the lives of others while shining the spotlight on God."

— Holy Hustle, chapter 9 —

Read Hebrews 11

1. How many times does the phrase "by faith" appear in your translation of this passage?

2. Read verse 39. If you are in a season of waiting, or unsure why God is asking you to do the work you're doing, how does this verse offer comfort or hope?

Day 5

3. List anything from this week's readings that have encouraged you to work for God's glory instead of your own.

"God worked and called it good, and He rested and called it holy."

— Holy Hustle, chapter 10 –

Week 8

Lessons in Waiting.

There are many things that I'm good at, but waiting is not one of them. I make decisions quickly and expect to see results. I plan ahead to know how much time we'll need when we leave the house and get frustrated when I'm standing around wondering what everyone else is doing. I don't like to "trust the process."

It's easy for me to start striving instead of serving when things aren't moving at my preferred timeline. Anyone else? This week we'll explore what happens when we choose to wait on God, and how rest – like waiting – takes practice.

> *"No prophet has arisen again in Israel like Moses, whom the Lord knew face to face."*
> *Deuteronomy 34:10*

Who wrote the book of Deuteronomy?

When was it written?

What are the themes of Deuteronomy?

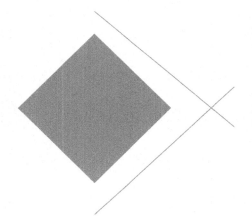

What do you hope to learn from our study this week?

Day 2

Read Deuteronomy 32:45 - 34:10 again (if you'd like, choose a different translation to see if it helps you focus if this is a familiar passage).

1. What do you initially take away from your reading today?

2. What does this section of Scripture teach us about God?

Day 2

3. How does this Scripture come alive in a new way as you read it through a "holy hustle" lens?

Lessons in Waiting
Deuteronomy 32:45 – 34:10

In order to read all that happened in Moses's life you would need to start in Exodus 2 and read through our final verse today. Moses experienced the glory of God like no one else on earth. He walked with Him, talked with Him, relayed messages and commandments from Him. He spent so much time with God that his face would shine afterward.

Moses knew that God had promised to rescue the Israelites from Egypt and provide a promised land, but Moses wouldn't be allowed to enter. In Numbers 20:11 we read that, instead of trusting God and waiting on Him, Moses took it upon himself to bring water out of a rock. And so, at the end of his life, he was allowed to see the land God promised, but he never entered with his people.

All that time, all that wandering, and right when the promise was to be fulfilled, Moses couldn't be a part of it all.

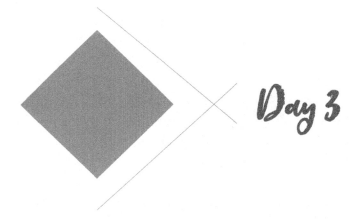

Read Joshua 1:1-5

1. How does this Scripture connect with what we read yesterday in Deuteronomy?

2. What connection have you seen in your own life between a struggle to wait and a struggle to rest?

Day 3

3. Consider the times that you have rushed ahead without waiting on God. What blessings do you think you have missed because you chose to do things your own way?

Joshua 1:5
CSB

"I will be with you, just as I was with Moses. I will not leave you or abandon you."

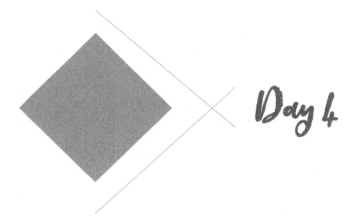

Day 4

Read Deuteronomy 32:45 - 34:10

1. Take a look at the final verses in chapter 34. Although
   Moses wasn't allowed to enter the promised land, what DID
   God do for him?

2. Put yourself in Moses's shoes for a moment and write down
   what these final moments of his life would have been like.
   What would he have seen? How would he have felt?

Day 4

3. How would your work-hard, rest-well life be different if you were able to stop pushing ahead with your own plans and learn, instead to rest and wait on God?

"If rest isn't too good for God, why do we act like we don't have time for it? "

— Holy Hustle, chapter 9 —

Day 5

Read Deuteronomy 32:45 - 34:10

1. What are your struggles when it comes to the idea of incorporating rest into your schedule?

2. We read in these verses that Moses not only worked hard for God's Kingdom, but took time to rest and be with Him as well. What kind of rest makes you feel connected with God AND rejuvenated?

Day 5

3. List anything from this week's readings that have encouraged you to wait faithfully on God.

"God has created us with such care that there should be no surprise our rest can be as unique as our work."

Holy Hustle, chapter 10

Lessons Learned

Use this space to record any holy hustle lessons you want to remember from this study.

_____

_____

_____

_____

_____

_____

_____

_____

_____

_____

_____

_____

_____

_____

Next Steps

On this page, take some time to set some holy hustle goals and next steps for yourself (and share with a friend to stay accountable!)

_____

_____

_____

_____

_____

_____

_____

_____

_____

_____

_____

_____

_____

_____

_____

_____

_____

_____

_____

Work without Shame, Rest without Guilt

Balance. It's what we long for in our lives as the world yells, "Work harder!" and the church demands, "Stop and rest." What if God's plan for us isn't just one way or the other?

Enter the *holy hustle*.

Crystal Stine followed the world's path to success as she climbed the corporate ladder. Now she's exploring "hustle" in a new light as a self-employed, work-from-home mom. She invites you to join her in experiencing...

renewed peace as you focus on serving, not striving

reawakened potential as you ditch comparison and embrace community

redefined purpose as you seek the roles God has for you

You were created to work with enthusiasm for the right reasons—and you were also made with a need to rest. Discover the place where these two sides meet in a happy, holy hustle.

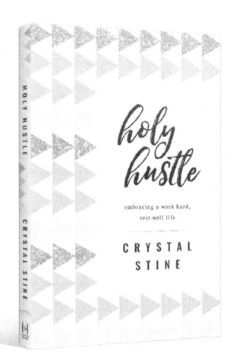

Available wherever books are sold.

Connect!

Instagram.com/crystalstine
www.crystalstine.me

**Sign up for 12 free holy hustle printables at
http://bit.ly/holyhustleemails**

Made in the USA
Monee, IL
26 September 2020